The Great Ancestor Hunt

❖ LILA PERL ❖

The Great Ancestor Hunt

❖

THE FUN OF FINDING
OUT WHO YOU ARE

DRAWINGS BY ERIKA WEIHS
ILLUSTRATED WITH PHOTOGRAPHS

CLARION BOOKS

NEW YORK

Acknowledgments and photo credits appear on page 101.

Clarion Books
a Houghton Mifflin Company imprint
215 Park Avenue South, New York, NY 10003
Text copyright © 1989 by Lila Perl
Drawings copyright © 1989 by Erika Weihs

Library of Congress Cataloging-in-Publication Data
Perl, Lila.
The great ancestor hunt.

Bibliography: p.
Summary: A guide for tracing one's ancestors via
various means. An appendix describes how to use a
number of available government resources.
1. Genealogy—Juvenile literature. [1. Genealogy]
I. Title.
CS15.5.P47 1989   929'.1'072   88-36211
ISBN 0-89919-745-0   PA ISBN 0-395-54790-3

Designed by Sylvia Frezzolini

CRW   20 19 18 17

TO MY FATHER,
Oscar Perl

In loving memory of my mother, Fay Rosenthal,
and my grandparents, Hannah and Joseph Perl,
and Sarah and Jacob Rosenthal

And for Diane, Kenneth,
Andrew, Ariane, and Jason

What's past is prologue.

—Shakespeare, *The Tempest*

❖❖❖❖ CONTENTS ❖❖❖❖

An old-fashioned family photo, taken in the days of stiff, formal studio portraits

ONE

Who Cares About Great-Uncle Edgar?

*W*e come across an old family photograph. The photo is in black and white, and it's faded and cracked. The person in the picture stands stiffly against a real or painted background of draperies, foliage, and elaborate furnishings.

This old-fashioned studio portrait was taken in the early 1900s. At that time, posing for one's photograph was a serious business. It meant "freezing" in front of the big, bulky studio camera for many seconds or even minutes. The quick, informal snapshots of today were still a rarity because small hand-held cameras had only recently been invented.

But who is this person in the picture? Is it your great-grandfather's brother, the first member of the family to become a famous brain surgeon, fondly and respectfully known to all as Great-Uncle Edgar? Or is it your great-grandfather himself, the most studious boy in his class, who sadly had to drop out of school to go to work and never fulfilled his dream of becoming a brilliant district attorney?

Here's another photo. Who are the two little girls, aged eight and ten, in their hair bows, sailor dresses, dark cotton stockings, and high-laced shoes? Would you be surprised to learn that they are your great-grandmother and her sister?

Can you see any family resemblance between you and the child your great-grandmother once was? Do you think your ambition to become a doctor or lawyer might have anything to do with the careers dreamed of by relatives who were growing up years ago?

Possibly you don't see any connection at all, and you're wondering why we should even care about our ancestors. Your great-

Could one of these two little girls in hair bows and high-laced shoes have been your great-grandmother?

grandparents may have died before you were born. Or, if they are alive, they may live in a distant place. The same may be true of your grandparents.

These days, it's easy to lose touch even with our own parents. They may have separated or divorced. One or both of them may have remarried, and we may find ourselves part of a step-family, with a whole new set of relatives. Or possibly we are being raised by just one parent. Many young Americans today can't even *name* all four of their parents' parents.

Yet, whether we know our ancestors or not, we are each a link in a human chain. We share our genes—the tiny units in our body cells that are responsible for inherited traits—with our forebears. And we'll pass on new combinations of these traits to our children and our children's children.

The word *genealogy*, which means the study of family lines of descent, comes from *gene*. Our genes are what determine the color of our eyes and hair, the shape of our bodies, the special workings of our brains. They are what give us our inborn talent for music, science, or sports. Even certain diseases, how long we will live, and what we will eventually die of may be traceable to our genes.

Scientists believe that there may be as many as thirty-five hundred inherited, or genetic, diseases. Some are as mild as a mere tendency toward hay fever. Others are as serious as hemophilia, in which the blood's failure to clot can lead to uncontrollable bleeding from even a tiny cut or scrape. In many cases, healthy parents are the carriers of the disease-causing genes. Some inherited illnesses are found in specific racial groups. Sickle-cell anemia strikes children of black families, while Tay-Sachs disease attacks Jewish infants of eastern European ancestry. Death in infancy or early childhood can result from such abnormalities of the genes.

On a happier note, we can also inherit a trait such as great musical talent from our ancestors. An amazing example is found in the family of the famous composer Johann Sebastian Bach. Bach's earliest-known musical ancestor was born in the late 1500s. Forty out of sixty of this ancestor's descendants, many of whom lived during the 1700s, became accomplished and even outstanding musicians!

Heredity — the Bach "bloodline" — was an important factor in producing so much musical talent. But was it the only reason? The various Bach-family children all grew up in strongly disciplined, music-centered households. Their surroundings helped their inborn abilities to blossom. Similar abilities in children who were not exposed to music may have withered because their talents were never encouraged.

In other words, our home, our schooling, the time and place in which we live are all important influences on how we develop. They form part of what we call our environment. It isn't merely sharing certain genes that accounts for similarities among family members. We often are alike because of our shared experiences.

Adopted children, for example, may be closer in mannerisms, attitudes, and even appearance to their adoptive family than to their natural, or biological, family. They "take after" their adoptive parents — to whom they have no "blood" ties — because of close family ties, or environment.

Heredity or environment, which links us more closely to our living, and even dead, ancestors? The answer is probably a combination of the two. You may grow up to have the tall, broad-shouldered build and prematurely white hair of your great-great-grandfather. That's heredity.

If, on the other hand, your great-great-grandfather hadn't courageously crossed the Atlantic as a young man nearly one hundred years ago — and soon sent for your great-great-grandmother and their two-year-old daughter (your great-grandmother) — would you be living in America today? In having left the poverty and

RIGHT: *A great-great-grandmother who fled her tiny Russian village for America.* LEFT: *A great-grandmother — her daughter — as a young woman posing for her engagement photograph*

fearful uncertainties of life in a tiny European village, your great-great-grandparents changed not only their own environment. They changed yours as well.

❖

Who were the very first people to keep records of their family lines and why? People have been searching for their "roots," constructing their "family trees" ever since earliest times. They have done so out of curiosity, a sense of family pride, and often, too, to establish inheritance claims. For, by tradition, rights of rulership, land holdings, and other possessions have been handed down from parent to child.

Even before they kept written records, many peoples relied on oral history to recall their ancestors. This was true among the ancient Scandinavians, Irish, Scots, and Welsh. Storytellers and poet-singers known as bards passed on the names and heroic deeds of dozens of earlier generations to younger members of the clan or tribe, to be memorized for safekeeping. We think of a generation as the time span between *our* being born and the birth of our children — usually twenty-five to thirty years. But there have been — and still are — peoples among whom a new generation was produced as often as every fifteen to twenty years.

Among certain Africans, Indonesians, and Pacific islanders, oral history is still very much alive. In recent times, a chieftain of the Maori, the Polynesian people native to New Zealand, recited a thirty-four-generation history of his people as a claim to the inheritance of a certain piece of territory in that country. His recital was said to have taken three days!

The lengthiest oral history ever delivered is reported to have covered *seventy* generations. It was offered by an old man on a small Indonesian island off the coast of Sumatra, in the Indian Ocean. Island people are among the most likely to have spoken records that go back so far. One reason is that it's easier to keep track of one's family history in a confined area. Another is that land is in short supply on an island, so the inheritance rights passed (in most cases) from father to son have to be clearly spelled out.

By contrast, the Native Americans of the territory that is today the United States and Canada were few in number compared with the large land mass they occupied. They didn't think in terms of land ownership. And so, although American Indians

The children of a Kiowan Indian chief of long ago, two sisters and a baby in a cradleboard. Native American families were among those who recalled their ancestors through oral history.

❖ 7

recalled their ancestry through oral history, they seldom went back more than five or six generations.

Oral history endures, of course, only as long as it is both remembered and retold. Otherwise it dies. In 1966, a group of high school English students in Rabun Gap, Georgia, began to interview the Appalachian mountain people among whom they lived. Many, in fact, were elderly members of the students' own families. Under the guidance of their teacher, Eliot Wigginton, the students published a magazine called *Foxfire*. It contained the spoken rememberings of the mountain dwellers.

As the wealth of material grew, the magazine developed into a numbered series of best-selling *Foxfire* books, covering traditional crafts and skills—from banjo making to bear hunting—stories, songs, and other mountain lore. *Foxfire* not only preserved the rich heritage of a fast-disappearing segment of American life. It also enriched the young people who collected the folkways of the southern Appalachians. And it gave rise to many similar projects throughout the country.

Probably the most famous personal experience with oral history in our time is the one that Alex Haley wrote about in his book *Roots: The Saga of an American Family.* Haley's story, which was published in 1976, described what he learned as a result of his amazingly successful search for his African ancestry.

Haley's first slave ancestor, as revealed in *Roots*, was a man named Kunta Kinte, who had been brought to America in the 1760s. During Haley's childhood years, his grandmother had told him stories she had heard as a child about a man called "Kintay" who'd been kidnapped by slavers near the "Kamby Bolongo" in Africa and taken by ship to a place called "Naplis" in the United States. There he was sold to a plantation owner who brought him to work in Virginia, under the slave name of Toby.

The spoken memories of Haley's grandmother made a deep impression on him. As a grown man, he began a twelve-year search for his roots. "Naplis," he discovered, was Annapolis, a port city in Maryland, while the "Kamby Bolongo" was the Gambia River in the West African country of Gambia. Learning that there were tribal historians in Gambia known as *griots*, Haley traveled to that country. There, a *griot* recited for Haley the history of his family, the Kinte clan, tracing the line all the way back to the time of Kunta Kinte's grandfather in the early 1700s.

Using the oral histories told him by both his grandmother and

A black settler family in front of their sod house on the Nebraska plains

the *griot*, Haley later found, from old shipping records, the name of the ship that had brought Kunta Kinte to the New World. He even uncovered the two-hundred-year-old deed showing the name of the owner of his slave ancestor. Like the pieces of a puzzle, the story of Haley's family all seemed to come together. Not only did it reinforce black family pride. It was an inspiration to all Americans who wanted to learn more about their family backgrounds, no matter how humble.

❖

The people who kept the first *written* records of their ancestry were probably the ancient Egyptians and the Chinese. Such records were especially important to the wealthier classes in these civilizations because they had the most to gain through inheritance. At the very top of the heap were the royal families, known as dynasties, that ruled in both Egypt and China for thousands of years. Enormous power and untold wealth were bestowed on the members of those noble family lines.

Among the Chinese, the common people, too, kept detailed family records. This was because the devotion of sons to fathers and the worship of ancestors were important parts of the teachings of Confucius, a Chinese philosopher who lived twenty-five hundred years ago. Confucianism spread through all levels of Chinese society. Even the poorest homes had altars inscribed with the names of ancestors. It was the duty of the eldest son in the family to burn incense and make offerings at the altar.

In religions like those of ancient Greece and Rome, the gods themselves had complete family trees. In fact, they were much like earthly royal families, to whom they were sometimes "related." Romulus and Remus, the founders of Rome, were said to be the twin sons of Mars, the Roman god of war. While the story of Rome's founding is a legend, many *real* earthly rulers, over the centuries, have claimed godly or other kinds of glorious ancestors.

In this century, an African monarch, Emperor Haile Selassie of Ethiopia, claimed to trace *his* ancestry all the way back to the Old Testament, which is also called the Hebrew Bible. When he was crowned in 1930, Haile Selassie declared himself to be the 225th ruler of the hereditary line that started with the union of King Solomon and the Queen of Sheba.

The Bible itself, beginning with Adam and Eve, often reads like a vast family history. The words *bore* and *begot* spring from many of its pages, as the family lines of biblical characters are described along with their deeds and teachings.

As European society developed, from the Middle Ages onward, members of the upper classes often referred to their family history as their "pedigree." Today this word makes us think of some prize-winning animal, like a carefully bred racehorse, a blue-ribbon bull, or a fancy show poodle. Actually, the word *pedigree* comes from the Middle French *pie de grue*, meaning "foot of a crane." This is because, on old genealogy charts, the lines showing who was descended from whom formed a pattern resembling the shape of a crane's foot.

The idea that pedigrees were only for the elite persisted until fairly recent times. Most people wouldn't have presumed to draw up an impressive-looking chart showing their ancestry. They felt that if they couldn't trace their family back to a duke, an earl, or some other titled person, they didn't have anything to be especially proud of. In England, one of the acid tests for proving that you had important family connections was to find your ancestor's name in an old, old volume called the Domesday Book.

The crowded tenement room of a New York City immigrant family of the early 1900s, too poor and struggling to dream of having a family "pedigree"

This first official record of many of England's early landowners was put together shortly after William the Conquerer, a French duke, invaded England in the year 1066. After taking much territory away from its owners and giving it to his followers, William ordered the preparation of the Domesday Book. Completed in 1086, it contained a detailed listing of the names of the new landed gentry and the size of their estates.

If *Domesday* looks similar to *doomsday*, the reason is that it comes from that word, is usually pronounced that way, and often meant the same thing. For, a landowner whose name did *not* appear in the Domesday Book had lost all legal rights to his property. On the other hand, having your name inscribed in the Domesday Book made you a member of the early English aristocracy. Your descendants would always look back to you with pride at being able to trace such a long family line.

In America, searching for an illustrious ancestor didn't become fashionable until the 1800s. Once the Revolutionary War period was over, some Americans who had begun to enjoy increased wealth started to look around for a way to add to their family's dignity. One mark of distinction was to be able to say that you were descended from a passenger who had arrived on the *May-flower*, the ship that carried the first Pilgrims to America in 1620. Another was to trace your roots to one of the "first families of Virginia," which became a colony of the English king in 1624.

Being related to a signer of the Declaration of Independence or to someone who fought in the American Revolution was also a great honor for a family to claim. Some of the tracings of wealthy Americans seeking a glorious past tended to be a little fuzzy, though. And a few individuals made real blunders. Imagine trying to get anyone to believe that you were a direct descendant of George Washington. History tells us that the famous "father of his country" never had any children of his own!

It was probably to help set the record straight about being related to a *Mayflower* passenger that the Society of Mayflower Descendants was formed in 1897. As nearly half of the 102 Mayflower Pilgrims had died by the autumn of 1621, many had no offspring. After the society came into existence, firm proof was required for claiming descent from any of the *Mayflower* passengers who did have children. Similarly, the Daughters of the American Revolution was organized in 1890 for women who could prove direct descent from patriots who had aided the cause of American independence.

As newly rich American families began to cast around for glowing pedigrees, a variety of genealogy specialists turned up to help provide them. Many researchers tried their best to be honest and accurate. But some told people what they wanted to hear — that they were closely related to European royalty or were the missing heirs to a great fortune. Looking for glamorous family connections could be tiresome, disappointing, and also quite costly. All too often, the "English duke" who was supposed to have been your great-great-grandfather turned out to have been a chimney sweep. Those stately, noble Venetians you'd hoped you were descended from were really a long line of barbers.

An event that helped change the way ordinary, everyday Americans thought about their family backgrounds was the 1976 Bicentennial. This two hundredth anniversary of the signing of the Declaration of Independence celebrated the birth of the United States.

People from other lands had been arriving on America's shores even before the time of the *Mayflower*. But the greatest flow of immigrants to the United States had taken place in the years between 1880 and 1920. A large percentage of Americans in the Bicentennial birthday period were the children, grandchildren, and great-grandchildren of those immigrants. They felt that this was a time for looking back as well as ahead, for tracing the way they had come. Others, whose families had been in America longer — as well as those who had arrived more recently — were also caught up in the great ground swell of interest in family origins.

An Italian family arriving in America during the great wave of immigration that took place between 1880 and 1920

Americans began to realize that everyone—not just people who were trying to come up with a notable pedigree—had a family history. Alex Haley's discovery of his African ancestors served as a perfect example. And, by happy coincidence, his book *Roots* was published in the very year of America's Bicentennial. Soon afterward, Haley's story was presented as a TV miniseries that was seen by a vast audience, and the book itself was translated into more than forty languages.

Today most of us go ancestor hunting because we both appreciate and are proud of the struggles and achievements of the earlier generations of our family. At the same time, getting to know our origins gives us a sense of stability in an uncertain and rapidly changing world. Finding out where we came from can help to explain and clarify the present, and may make it easier to focus on the future.

Ancestor hunting offers us a kind of "time travel," too. As we search out the lives of earlier family members, we are transported into their world, as it existed before we were born. We find that every family has its oral history, in the form of personal stories and shared experiences that have a special flavor. Many families, too, have letters, diaries, and other writings that are rich samplings of who our forebears were and how they reacted to the times and places in which they lived. And old family pictures —even stiff portraits and blurry black-and-white snapshots— can be "worth a thousand words" as they unreel the past like a movie run backward.

Today many young people find themselves getting involved in family-history projects in schools, libraries, and museums. At a recent "heritage fair" at a junior high school, participants ranged from those whose families had come to America in colonial times to immigrants who had arrived in the United States only months earlier.

In addition to drawings of family trees and ancestor charts, the students brought in samples of family memorabilia to display. Their "mini museum" included a great-great-grandmother's flat-iron from Massachusetts in the 1800s, a great-grandmother's hand-decorated poetry notebook brought from Finland, and a grand-parents' photo showing them as Brooklyn teenagers in the 1940s! Newer Americans contributed a great-grandfather's shepherd's vest from Greece, a silver baby-feeding cup from India, and an old wooden abacus from China. Each object opened a door and

A black-and-white snapshot that vividly takes us to an earlier time, like a movie run backward

told a story. It served as a key to what made each family and each person in it special.

Looking back at our origins, we are reminded that, had we never been born, our families could very well have existed without us. But *we* could not have come to be without them. So perhaps, in a way, we owe it to our ancestors — as well as to the generations that will come after us — to care about Great-Uncle Edgar and other seemingly long-lost relatives who are a vital part of our family line.

Each of us can be an important link between the past and the future. In closing the generation gap that separates our grandparents from our grandchildren, we can actually span five or six lifetimes. An adventure in itself, this is only part of the fun of finding out who we are!

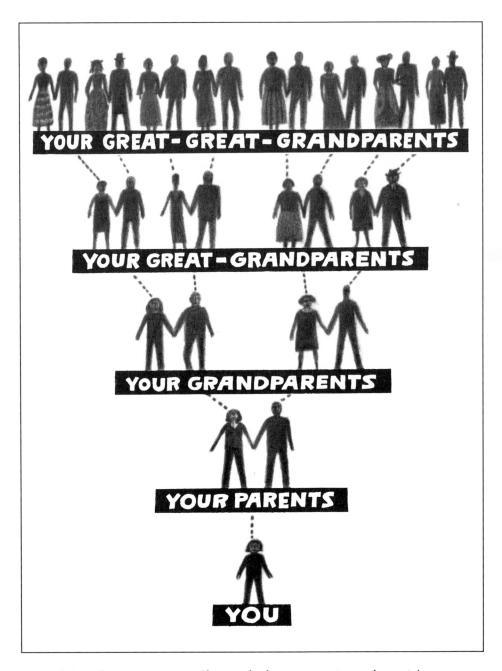

We each have fourteen ancestors if we go back to our great-grandparents' generation, and thirty if we reach even farther back to our great-great-grandparents.

TWO

Tracing Your Family's Roots

So we're going to start hunting for information about our ancestors. Where do we begin? Do we pick out the most faded photograph in our family album and try to learn more about the person in the picture? Do we choose the oldest living relative in our family and start asking questions?

Logical as those approaches may seem, the answer is no. We start just the opposite way around—with ourselves. We work backward, going from the known to the unknown, from our generation to that of our parents, then to that of our grandparents, and so on.

Suppose we dig successfully for roots going all the way back to our great-grandparents. We'll have discovered some fascinating facts about fourteen people in our direct family line. If we go back one more generation to our great-great-grandparents, there will be thirty names, aside from our own, on our ancestors' chart.

Notice how the numbers jump. Since it takes two persons to make one person, going back six generations would give us 126 ancestors; going back ten would give us over 2,000!

We need to remember, though, that in earlier times people seldom traveled far from their own villages. So, many marriages took place between fairly close relatives, such as first or second cousins. This meant that a married couple would share certain family members through both blood and marriage, and their children would have fewer forebears.

Among the royalty of ancient Egypt, even brothers and sisters were known to marry each other in order to keep wealth and power in the family. As a result, *their* children had only one set of grandparents instead of the usual two. So, if you *could* trace your family back ten generations or more, you might find that you didn't have quite as many ancestors as the mathematical tables say.

Getting back to your own generation, you may be surprised at how much information you already have about yourself, even if you are still fairly young. And since you probably have family members around to help you, further information should be quite easy to obtain. A good way to start working on your roots is to try writing down the answers to the following questions:

· What is your full name, including first, middle, and last names?

· What is your date of birth? Where were you born?

· How did your parents, or parent, choose your first name and your middle name, if you have one? If you were named after a relative, who was it? Is that person still alive?

· What can you find out about your last name, which is

also called a family name or surname? Do you know what country it comes from? Does it mean anything special? Was it ever changed from some other surname? How or why?

· What are your parents' full names? Do you know what your mother's family name is? After marriage, this is referred to as a maiden name. Does your mother still use her own family name, as many women do?

· Do you have any sisters or brothers, and what are their names and ages?

· In what places have you lived? What schools have you gone to? What are your special interests? What are the most memorable events of your life so far?

Before too much more time goes by, you might even want to make up a chart called a personal time-line. A time-line is a way of diagraming your life from birth to the present. You can use photographs or drawings, or just written entries, to show the highlights of each year. A time-line is a little like an illustrated diary. Later, when you talk to older members of your family, you'll wish they had done the same when they were your age. If you start now, your own children and grandchildren will be forever grateful to you. Time-lines, personal scrapbooks, photo albums with detailed notations, and day-by-day written diaries are all valuable clues that help make the work of an ancestor hunter both exciting and rewarding.

❖

There are a great many questions about names — first, last, and middle — among the facts to set down about ourselves. Perhaps you're wondering why. The answer is that names are keys to our identity. Suppose you were given the same first or middle name as an older relative, one who was either living or dead at the time of your birth. Why was that name chosen for you? What can you find out about the person whose namesake you are? The name you share with one of your forebears may help you discover your first truly revealing link to the past.

In some cases, given names are changed as they are handed down. You may be called Brooke after your great-grandmother whose name was Belle. Or Lindsay after a grandfather who was known as Louis. Foreign names may be converted into English — Dimitrios into James, Esteban into Steven. In some families, children are named after parents or other living relatives. In

A personal time-line is like an illustrated diary that shows . . .

certain Jewish families, it is against religious custom to pass on the name of any but the dead. But no matter what pattern has been followed, asking questions about your first and middle names may bring to light an interesting bit of family history.

Surnames, or second names, can tell us even more about our roots. Today it's hard to imagine a time when no second names existed. But centuries ago in England, for example, dozens of people in a small village would have been called simply John (or Ann or Robert or Katherine or Henry). Imagine how confusing this became back in the 1200s, before England passed laws ordering people to take family names. How could one tell all the Johns apart? There was John who was the son of William; there was John the baker; there was John who lived down at the waterside; and then there was John who was very, very short—to mention just a few.

the highlights of your life from birth to the present.

Actually, identifying people by the names of their parents, by the kind of work they did, by where they lived, or by what they looked like turned out to be a pretty good idea. By the 1400s, when people were required by English law to register their surnames, our various "Johns" simply would have had themselves listed as John Williamson, John Baker, John Atwater, and John Short.

In America today, most family names can be traced to one of these four categories: parent's names, occupations, place names, and descriptive names. Surnames like Johnson (and Jones), Richardson, Davison, and Peters all tell us that the first person to record that name was a son of John, Richard, David, or Peter. Nor was it only the English who chose patronymics, or fathers' first names, as the source of family names. The *Mc*, *Mac*, and *Fitz* in Irish and Scottish names like McHugh, MacGregor, and Fitzgerald all mean "son of" Hugh, Gregory, or Gerald. And the *O'* in the Irish O'Brien stands for "descendant of" Brien. A little harder to recognize is the Welsh *ap*, or "son of," put before a father's name like Evan or Owen. But if you say "ap Evan" or "ap Owen" quickly, you won't be surprised to learn that they were the origins of Welsh surnames like Bevan and Bowen.

Patronymic family names are found among many other national groups. The German Mendelssohn is "son of Mendel," while the Scandinavian Martensen is "son of Martin." Adamovich is Russian for "son of Adam," Antonopoulos is Greek for "son of Anton," the Italian di Giovanni means (son) "of John," and the *ez* in Fernandez gives this Spanish name its meaning of "son of Fernando."

Didn't people ever register surnames that came from their mothers instead of their fathers? The answer is yes, but not nearly so often. Names like Anson, Allison, Margeson, and Nelson all seem to be matronymics, meaning they were taken from mothers' first names such as Ann, Alice, Margaret, and Nell. But notice that they all end with *son*. There are only rare cases of either patronymic or matronymic surnames ending with *daughter*. Some examples from the Scandinavian countries would be Gunnarsdatter (daughter of a father named Gunnar) and the even rarer all-female name Kristinsdatter (meaning the daughter of a mother named Kristin).

Have you ever wondered why Smith is the most common family name in the United States, as well as in a number of other places? The answer is quite simple. Being a smith — a worker in metals, especially iron — was the most widespread occupation back in the days when surnames were first being recorded. Blacksmiths not only shod horses. They made and mended plows and all sorts of farming and household tools. They created suits of armor and weapons of war. Without the work of the smiths, neither the lords nor the peasants could have gone about their pursuits.

Other surnames that come directly from occupations tell us what else people were working at during the Middle Ages. So, of course, we have Miller, Baker, Farmer, Shepherd, Fisher, Carpenter, Mason, Sawyer, Barber, Taylor (tailor), Carter (cart driver), Clark (clerk), and many, many more.

Surnames like Goldsmith and Arrowsmith are variations of Smith. They were taken by craftspeople who specialized in gold work or arrow making. But the reason for the overwhelming number of just plain Smiths in the United States is that many foreign names that meant "smith," as a worker in iron, were translated into English. Here is just a partial list of "Smiths" in their original languages: Schmidt (German), Smit (Dutch), Le Fevre (French), Ferraro (Italian), Herrera (Spanish), Kuznetsov (Russian), Kowalski (Polish), Kovar (Czech), Kovacs (Hungarian), and Haddad (Syrian).

So it's not surprising that one out of every one hundred Amer-

Surnames from Parents' Names		Surnames from Occupations	
Johnson	Antonopoulos	Smith	Fisher
McHugh	di Giovanni	Miller	Carpenter
O'Brien	Fernandez	Baker	Barber
Mendelssohn	Nelson	Farmer	Taylor
Adamovich	Kristinsdatter	Shepherd	Carter

Over 30 percent of the family names that originated in the British Isles and Europe were taken from parents' first names, and about 15 percent come from peoples' occupations.

icans today is a Smith. And that doesn't include the one hundred thousand or so others who spell their names with variations like Smyth, Smythe, Smithe, Schmitt, Schmitz, Smits, and so on! Whichever way we may prefer to spell our occupational surnames, they are fascinating clues to our ancestors and the roles they played in providing the necessities of everyday life in a time long past.

Place names like Atwater (used to identify John who lived "at the water") are the largest source of surnames in English. Woods, Meadows, Fields, Rivers, Brooks, Lane, Poole, Lake, Marsh, and Grove are only some of the almost unending number of "landscape" names. The most popular of all English names taken from nature is Hill. And names meaning "mountain" pop up in many foreign tongues, as in the German and Scandinavian Berg and the French DuMont ("of the mountain"). Other common landscape names include the Spanish del Río ("of the river"), the Italian Campi ("fields"), and the Polish Borowski ("of the woods").

The structures in or near which our ancestors dwelt gave us surnames like Lodge, Mills, Bridges, Church, and Castle. As larger communities developed, some people took their family names from town names, adding variations so they wouldn't all sound alike. Later, when people began to move greater distances, and especially to emigrate to America, they took the names of cities in Europe where they had been born or perhaps had sailed from, like London, Berlin(er), or Hamburg(er). Polish and Russian immigrants named Warshauer, Minsky, or Moscowitz probably came from Warsaw, Minsk, or Moscow. Italians named Genovese or Napoli were from Genoa or Naples.

Short, Stout, and Small, as well as Longfellow, Armstrong,

Hardy, and Fairchild, are all descriptive surnames based on the general appearance of some long-lost ancestor. The most common of all such names is Brown. Like Black, White, Gray, and Reid (for "red"), these names refer to skin tone or hair color. Keen, Meek, Moody, Merriman, Sweet, and Goodfriend describe

Surnames from Place Names	
Hill	Bridges
Atwater	Church
Woods	Berliner
Rivers	Minsky
Marsh	Genovese

Surnames from Descriptive Names	
Short	Meek
Longfellow	Moody
Armstrong	Merriman
Fairchild	Sweet
Brown	Goodfriend

Place names are the source of 43 percent of surnames in English, while descriptive names make up almost 10 percent of such family names.

personal qualities. And many such names are found in foreign languages as well. Klein is German for "small"; LeBrun is French for "the brown one"; Pokorny, meaning "meek," is found in Slavic tongues; and so on.

What are the five most frequently occurring names in the United States today? They are Smith, Johnson, Williams, Brown, and Jones, in that order. Three of them are from fathers' first names, one is occupational, and one is descriptive. But there are many other popular American surnames that don't fit into any of these three groups, nor are they true place names.

Cohen, the second most common name in New York City after Smith, comes from the word *priest*. It was first taken by the descendants of Aaron, an ancient Hebrew high priest. Like Smith, it has numerous spellings, including Cone, Kohn, Cahn, and Kahan. Levy, another Jewish surname of very early origin, comes from the Levites, a tribe of important temple servants. Levi, Levin, Levine, and even Halevy ("the Levite") are popular variations.

But most Jewish surnames were "made up" sometime during the 1800s. This is when the officials in the central and eastern European countries where many Jews lived required that all Jews be registered. By tradition, Jews often went by names like Abraham ben ("son of") Jacob. In turn, Abraham's son Ezra would be known as Ezra ben Abraham, and Ezra's son David was David ben Ezra. This business of last names changing with each generation was very confusing for record keeping and wouldn't do at all. It's been reported that Jews often paid a sum of money to register an attractive-sounding family name like Rosenthal ("rose valley") or Goldblatt ("gold leaf"). Those who couldn't afford to pay might be given an ugly-sounding name such as Ochsenmaul ("ox's mouth") or Eselskopf ("ass's head") by a mean official.

These and other difficult-sounding and hard-to-spell foreign surnames were often changed by immigration officers at the time of their owners' arrival on American soil. Sometimes names were shortened; sometimes they were replaced entirely. Feinstein might simply become Fine; Teitelbaum ("date palm tree") might be transformed into the totally different but easier-to-spell . . . Greenberg! Most poor immigrants of the early 1900s were so pleased to be admitted to the United States that they hardly noticed or cared what name had been assigned to them. Part of the fascination of ancestor hunting is to try to find out what our earliest family names were, and if and why they were ever changed.

Like Jewish surnames, most Japanese surnames were also "made up" in the 1800s to obey an official decree that every family be registered. They, too, are not *real* place names but are meant to sound attractive, like Yamashita (which means "mountain, below"), Matsumoto ("pine, origin"), and Tanaka ("rice field, middle").

By contrast, the people of China first took surnames well over two thousand years ago at their emperor's command. Some historians say they were ordered to pick names from the words found in a short poem. This would explain why there are only about sixty popular Chinese names for such a large population and why they have such varied meanings as Chan ("old"), Fu ("teacher"), Wing ("warm"), and Lee ("pear tree"). Among the Chinese, and some other peoples as well, last names appear first and first names last, as in Lee Wah. But most Chinese-Americans have reversed their names to conform to the American custom, so Lee Wah becomes Wah Lee.

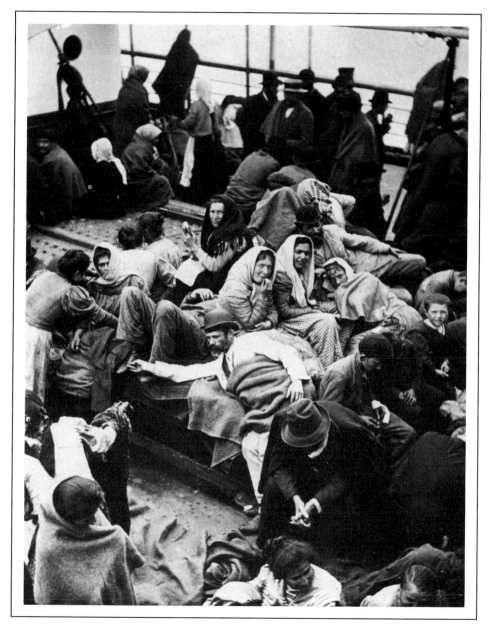

Among these European immigrant passengers of the early 1900s, about to dock in the United States, many will have the spellings and even the meanings of their names changed by immigration officers.

Among two groups—American Indians and blacks—there was almost no tradition of family names. American Indian names often described personal traits, deeds of bravery, admired animals, memorable events, even dreams. In many cases, men and women changed their names during their lifetime, as they matured and had new experiences. In some Indian groups, all the relatives of a person who had died were required to change *their* names. This may have been thought to be a way of shielding family members from death or misfortune. So family lines were very difficult to trace. It wasn't until after the United States government began to herd the Indians onto reservations and to send Indian children to school that surnames were chosen and registered. Some Indians took descriptive names like Eagle Feather, Red Bird, or Yellow Wolf as their family names, either in English or in the original Indian language. Others took names that didn't sound Indian at all. There were many variations because the whole idea of *having* a surname was foreign to Native American culture.

Similarly, few African peoples had handed-down surnames. And, on arriving in the United States, they almost always lost their African given names as well. Slave owners casually renamed them Sam, Joe, Sally, or whatever was easiest. Before the Civil War, if a slave used a surname, it was likely to be that of the white family he or she worked for. Since slave families were often split up and sold to different owners, it wasn't surprising that close relatives had different "family" names.

After the slaves were freed, most officially chose the white Southern names that were familiar to them, although not necessarily those of their former masters. Johnson is the most popular black surname in the United States today, and Brown is second. Others are Jackson, Jones, Robinson, and Williams. These reflect the fact that most white settlers in the American South were originally from the British Isles—and had gotten *their* surnames back in the 1400s when it had become too confusing to try to tell people apart from their first names only!

❖

Why *has* there been all this fuss about surnames over the centuries? The answer is that governments had long been looking for an easier and more efficient way of keeping track of people. Family names served as a sort of anchor and were useful to the authorities for all sorts of record keeping.

About five thousand years ago, long before surnames, the public officials of the Babylonians and the ancient Egyptians were already counting noses. And both the Old and New Testaments of the Bible offer examples of people being tallied. The reasons were almost always so that rulers could know how many men were available for military service *and* how much money they could expect to collect from their subjects in taxes.

It was the ancient Romans who gave the name *census* to these head counts. The very word *census* comes from the Latin *censere*, meaning to assess, or tax. Although censuses were hated and feared by the populace, more and more governments around the world adopted them. England's Domesday Book, issued in the year 1086, was really a census of the landowners of the day for the purpose of imposing taxes and also recruiting fighting men in the event of war. As surnames were not yet in use, the owners were identified by their titles and by the names, locations, and sizes of their landholdings.

Once people *had* second names, census takers had a much easier job. The first federal census in the United States took place in 1790, as provided for in the Constitution. And there has been a national census taken every ten years ever since. In addition to the usual reasons for census taking, the new government had a special need for knowing the exact size and distribution of its population. As a democracy, in which all citizens were to be represented, the government would have to determine how many members each state was entitled to elect to the House of Rep-

A vast job for the door-to-door census takers of 1910 was recording information about the dense population of congested areas like New York City's "Little Italy."

resentatives. Unfortunately, in the days when slavery still existed in the United States, black slaves were counted as only three-fifths of a person in the government's census. And many American Indians were not counted at all before 1860.

In the 1790 census, only heads of families — most of whom were men — were listed by their full names, along with their occupations. Wives and other women who were not heads of families, children, boarders, servants, and slaves were simply entered as part of the household. The main purpose was to divide the slaves from the free, and to find out how many males were over sixteen and available for military duty. The ages of other household members weren't recorded until the 1800 census, and then only roughly by groups, such as "under 10," "10 to 15," "16 to 25," "26 to 44," and so on.

From 1850 on, though, more and more information was taken in the census, such as the names of all household members, their exact ages and places of birth, and their occupations. This information began to make census records really helpful to government planners, concerned about the educational, social, and economic needs of the growing population, and to individuals tracing their family backgrounds on American soil. Such records would have been much harder both to compile and to make use of if surnames didn't exist.

As official as government censuses may look, however, it's a good idea to remember that they are often sprinkled with inaccuracies. Since earliest times, people have had a fear of being counted because taxes and/or death (through being sent to war) frequently seemed to result. There were also those who believed that counting the "wealth" of the land was a way of tempting evil and would be followed by disaster.

A 1940 census taker in Alaska, where the population was small compared with the large territory to be covered

A biblical example of such a calamity is found in the second book of Samuel in the Old Testament, or Hebrew Bible. It tells how King David of Israel set about counting all the men of fighting age in Israel and Judah. The able young men in the kingdom added up to a considerable number. But only a short time after the count had been completed, the land was visited by a terrible plague that killed seventy thousand of them. Was there a connection? Was the Bible story a warning that allowing oneself to be counted could lead to death?

36 ❖

Whatever their reason, some people have always hidden from the census taker, given vague or misleading answers, lied about their ages out of vanity, or been otherwise dishonest. And back in the days of door-to-door counts—before the advent of mail-in questionnaires—the census takers themselves didn't always get all the answers right. Nevertheless, census records can be a valuable source of "bare bones" family information, and are used extensively by professional genealogists.

Have you ever thought about being your own "family census taker"? What better way than to make up what genealogists call a direct-ancestry chart? And what easier way to start than by collecting basic facts about births, marriages, and deaths from your parents and other relatives?

At first, all the boxes and blank spaces on even a four-generation direct-ancestry chart may appear rather intimidating. But, on drawing up a rough copy of such a chart, you will find the first box—your own—easy to fill in. The same should be true for the boxes of the next generation, that of your parents. Genealogy experts advise, though, that you use pencil at first, as there are always some corrections to be made. And they suggest writing dates as "21 Sept 1944," or "6 June 1962" so there'll be no danger of jumbling the day, month, and year.

Once you start digging for information about your family, one thing is sure to lead to another. Pretty soon, someone is likely to say, "You really should ask Great-Aunt Martha or Great-Grandpa Harry about that." Or you may be referred to an older person who is outside the family. Often, a close family friend or neighbor of long standing will know a lot about your family

Four Generation Direct-Ancestry Chart

YOUR PARENTS

YOUR PARENTS

Your father's name
_____

DATE OF BIRTH
WHERE
DATE MARRIED
WHERE

YOU

Your name
_____

DATE OF BIRTH
PLACE OF BIRTH

Your mother's name*
_____

DATE OF BIRTH
WHERE
DATE MARRIED
WHERE

*her surname before marriage

*A four-generation direct-ancestry chart
with spaces for basic information about our
fourteen closest ancestors*

YOUR PATERNAL GRANDPARENTS

Your father's father's name
_____

BORN   WHERE
MARRIED   WHERE
DIED   WHERE

Your father's mother's name*
_____

BORN   WHERE
MARRIED   WHERE
DIED   WHERE

Your father's father's father's name
_____

BORN   WHERE
MARRIED   WHERE
DIED   WHERE

Your father's father's mother's name*
_____

BORN   WHERE
MARRIED   WHERE
DIED   WHERE

Your father's mother's father's name
_____

BORN   WHERE
MARRIED   WHERE
DIED   WHERE

Your father's mother's mother's name*
_____

BORN   WHERE
MARRIED   WHERE
DIED   WHERE

YOUR MATERNAL GRANDPARENTS

Your mother's father's name
_____

BORN   WHERE
MARRIED   WHERE
DIED   WHERE

Your mother's mother's name*
_____

BORN   WHERE
MARRIED   WHERE
DIED   WHERE

Your mother's father's father's name
_____

BORN   WHERE
MARRIED   WHERE
DIED   WHERE

Your mother's father's mother's name*
_____

BORN   WHERE
MARRIED   WHERE
DIED   WHERE

Your mother's mother's father's name
_____

BORN   WHERE
MARRIED   WHERE
DIED   WHERE

Your mother's mother's mother's name*
_____

BORN   WHERE
MARRIED   WHERE
DIED   WHERE

history. Now that you've been pointed in that direction, there's not much time to waste, for those whose memories go back the farthest have the fewest years left to them.

But sometimes we shy away from asking questions of older people. We feel that they are on the other side of a very wide "generation gap." Their answers may come hesitantly, or they may tire easily. Or they may tell us a long story about escaping from the old country or selling newspapers as a child when all we asked them was when and where they were born.

Rambling answers, though, are all to the good. A direct-ancestry chart, with its tiny spaces for nothing more than names, dates, and places, is really just a "family skeleton," a starting point. It's the stories about life in a New York City tenement or a journey in a covered wagon, about how a family fortune was lost or a romantic courtship flowered, that add flesh to the bare bones of our family's history.

We can interview older family members in a variety of ways. We can take written notes, use a tape recorder, or even make a videotape. Often, several short sessions are better than one long one. Between meetings, we may think of further questions to ask, and our relatives may think of new things to tell us. Bringing old family photographs along to an interview is a good idea. Older relatives are the most likely to be able to identify the people in the pictures. At the same time, the photos may jog their memories and bring forth a fresh avalanche of reminiscences.

Suppose the person whom "you really should talk to if you want to know about our family" lives too far away for you to meet with in person. It may be a relative you've never even heard of before. But how about writing a letter? Start out by introducing yourself and explaining that you are working on a family history. Make your questions short and to the point. Offer to share whatever else you learn, thank your relative in advance, and enclose a stamped, self-addressed envelope.

There are always some family members who prefer to keep what they know to themselves. But it is more than likely that you will get a response. You may even find that you have tapped into a rich new source of family information.

By now you surely will have made some progress with filling in the spaces on your direct-ancestry chart. How many generations before your own have you been able to go back? To that of your parents? Your grandparents? Your great-grandparents?

Can we go back to the generation of our great-great-grandparents, or does this feel like a tremendous leap into the past?

Can you go beyond the spaces on the four-generation chart to the generation of your great-great-grandparents? To complete a five-generation chart may seem a tremendous leap into the past. But it may not be as out of reach as it first appears. All you need to do to find out about your great-great-grandparents is to ask your grandparents what they remember about *their* grandparents!

Suppose, on the other hand, your chart is only partly filled in because some of your ancestral trails have reached an early dead

Great-great-grandparents seem easier to reach when we remember that they are our grandparents' grandparents. Here they pose in a 1904 photograph with their three young daughters, one of whom could have been your grandmother's mother.

end. Perhaps you live with only one parent and have lost contact with an entire branch of your family. Or, as an adoptee, your biological family is unknown to you. Remember that the closeness you share with your adoptive family makes its family history yours as well.

You are still part of the great ancestor hunt. The heritage of the family—or of those members of the family—that you live with is *your* heritage. And even if there is only one faint trail to follow into the past, you still have a very good chance of returning from your ancestor hunt with a fascinating family story to tell!

NOVA BRITANNIA.

OFFERING MOST

Excellent fruites by Planting in
VIRGINIA.

Exciting all such as be well affected
to further the same.

LONDON
Printed for SAMVEL MACHAM, and are to be sold at
his Shop in Pauls Church-yard, at the
Signe of the Bul-head.
1 6 0 9.

*A leaflet, dated 1609, intended to lure English planters to Virginia
and picturing a typical sailing vessel of the day*

THREE

Across the Ocean,
Over the Plains

*A*sk most people whose families have lived in the United States for a few generations what their national roots are. They probably will answer, "I'm an American."

It's fine to think of ourselves as being comfortable with and proud of the country in which we live. But the truth is that, whether your ancestors arrived by sailing ship in 1609 or you yourself stepped off a jet airplane just a few months ago, nearly all of us have come here from somewhere else. With the exception of the American Indians, we are all "immigrants." Some people might even argue that the Indians themselves are relative newcomers to the Americas. Many scientists date their arrival, via a land bridge from Asia, as having taken place a mere fifteen thousand years ago!

Asking questions about how our forebears first came to America is the way we begin to flesh out our family's story, to go beyond the bare facts that we've noted down on a direct-ancestry chart. There have been many writings, for example, that have described the hardships and dangers of months at sea on a storm-tossed sailing vessel. The passengers suffered from overcrowding, bad food, seasickness, and a lack of sanitary facilities. Even more horrifying were the conditions on the slave ships that sailed from Africa to the New World. Often the slaves were chained and confined to such small spaces that they could not stand up or even turn around. It was not unusual for more than half to die on the voyage and their bodies to be thrown overboard.

Eyewitness accounts of such sailings give us an idea of what sea travel was like for most people in the 1600s and 1700s. How did *your* immigrant relatives first reach these shores? In addition to *how* they traveled, you will also want to find out when and why. It has been said that each person's family history is really a reflection of world events, and that a family's story is actually history on a personal scale.

Suppose, for example, that your great-great-great-grandparents were living in Ireland at the time of the Irish potato famine. For generations the Irish farmers had depended on the potato for their daily food and as a crop to sell. But when the famine struck, more than one-quarter of the population of Ireland was forced to emigrate. Other European peoples may have been driven from their homelands by warfare or persecution. But *your* great-great-great-grandparents had to give up their old way of life because of . . . a deadly plant fungus.

The fringe of whitish fungus mold on the leaves of the potato plants first appeared in the fall of the year 1845. Nobody thought much of it. But a warm winter and a wet spring in 1846 caused the blight to spread. By summer the potato fields had turned into an evil-smelling black rot. The potatoes were inedible, and the "Great Famine" began to take its toll. One out of every six peasants starved to death. Many others joined the vast exodus to the New World that began late in 1846 and continued well into the 1850s.

The fleeing Irish traveled in the cargo holds of vessels bound for Canada or for the United States ports of New York or Boston. The cargo ships that carried them had no passenger cabins to speak of. But empty cargo spaces, far below deck, were fitted with makeshift wooden bunks covered with straw-stuffed mattresses. These crude accomodations—dark, dirty, and airless—

Fleeing victims of the Irish potato famine about to take passage for America

were known as steerage quarters because they usually were located in the rear, or steering, part of the vessel.

Most sea travel in the mid-1800s was just as uncomfortable and hazardous as it had been a hundred or two hundred years earlier. In fact, the Irish immigrants grimly referred to the vessels they sailed on as "coffin ships" because so many people died on the journey. Oceangoing steamships were only just being put into regular service. So most Atlantic crossings were made on the slower sail-driven ships. If an epidemic of typhus, cholera, or some other disease broke out, it could take many lives during the six or more weeks at sea. Fires, too, from candles, kerosene lamps, and cookstoves, were a great danger on board.

Once arrived in the New World, most of the potato-famine Irish tended to cluster in the slum quarters of coastal cities such as Boston and New York. They were too discouraged to try farming again, and most were penniless as well. So they found work mainly as street peddlers and day laborers. Later, many improved their lot and rose to higher positions, often in public services and city government. More than a million Irish immigrants came to America as a result of the 1840s potato famine alone. Is this the story of *your* ancestors, the "how, when, and why" of their arrival in the land your family has long called home?

A list of questions to ask an older relative about family origins can be helpful in eliciting stories like that of the potato-famine Irish. As the pieces come together, we will begin to see how the flow of past events has played an important role in determining the lives we live today. Leave plenty of time for the answers to these questions. Remember that rambling answers filled with colorful details are the ones that will most vividly recreate your family's background:

- · Who in our family first came to America? Do you know where they came from and when? What was their reason for leaving their country? How did they travel, and how long did it take?

- · What foreign port did they leave from, and where did they land?

- · Where in America did they first live, and what work did they do?

- · Where did they finally settle, and how did they travel there?

Perhaps the family story that you unearth will be one of crossing both the ocean and the American continent. Perhaps it will be the story of a pioneering journey in a covered wagon. Unlike those immigrants who remained in the coastal cities, many others soon struck out for the untamed lands of the interior. Usually, they moved by stages — settling, clearing land, farming, then pulling up stakes and setting off for new territory again. They might go from New England to western Pennsylvania or Ohio, then on to another frontier home in Indiana or Illinois. Finally, they might move on to Missouri to set out from one of its "jumping-off" points for the long overland trek by wagon to California or Oregon.

Between 1840 and 1870, over a quarter of a million Americans, mostly families, set off to cover the two thousand or so miles that led to the "gold country" and the rich farming lands of the

Pacific Coast. Many kept diaries. These records were meant to help others who might soon be making the often terrifying journey. People wrote of the hardships of living six to eight months on the trail in scorching heat and drenching rains, hailstorms, and even snowstorms. They told of fording rivers and hauling the wagons across the mountains. They spoke of the sicknesses and accidents that claimed the lives of both children and adults. Sadly, the dead had to be buried along the trail in lone graves left behind in the wilderness.

A covered-wagon family pauses as it crosses the inhospitable plains on the journey westward.

The diaries of the covered-wagon travelers also described everyday life on the trail—the monotonous diet of beans, biscuits, dried beef, and coffee; the search for fresh greens or for wild berries to bake in a pie at "nooning" when the wagons halted for a midday meal. The travelers' accounts told of those relatives who'd chosen to remain behind "back East," of the children who were born to the family along the way, and of the new homesteads that were built at the journey's end. Such writings were, in fact, family histories that recorded growth and change. Some were published or were collected by historical societies; others are still in family collections. Perhaps *your* family has the diary of a pioneer ancestor among its memorabilia. Or maybe an older relative can recall being told stories of a similar westward journey in his or her youth and can pass them on to you.

On the other hand, your family's first encounter with America may have come *after* the era of the covered wagon. Between 1880 and 1920, more immigrants entered the United States than in any other period—about 23 million of them. So there is a strong likelihood that you are descended from a forebear who traveled across the country on one of the newly built railroads rather than in a covered wagon.

From about 1870 on, railroads not only carried travelers to far-distant destinations in the United States; they began to offer them cheap land to settle on as well. The government had granted these lands to the railway companies to encourage them to build the rail lines. Now the companies were anxious to fill those barren acres with farms and cattle ranches, as well as towns and even small cities. Otherwise, there wouldn't be enough passengers and freight to carry to make the railroads' existence worthwhile.

So companies like the Union Pacific Railway and others began to advertise in European as well as American newspapers. If your great-great-grandfather lived in England, Germany, or Switzerland, in Holland or Scandinavia, he might have read such an ad or seen a poster in the window of a steamship company's office. The railroads often sent special agents abroad who also helped arrange for the ocean passages of the newcomers.

Such inducements, along with glowing letters from relatives already settled in America, caused many a European family to pull up its roots and set sail. As one new American wrote back to Norway, here was a land where hunger did not exist, where

A Union Pacific Railway poster designed to bring foreign settlers to the western lands along its route. The illustration at the right shows the Castle Garden immigration center in New York City; the picture at the left, a view of the Rocky Mountains.

52 ❖

one could "eat wheat bread every day and pork at least three times a week!" Of course, such reports often downplayed the hardships and discouragements that led some pioneering families to regret the decision they'd made. Life on the plains and in the territories beyond could be a succession of disasters caused by drought, blizzards, prairie fires, and insect plagues, to say nothing of illnesses, accidents, and unbearable loneliness. "In God we trusted, in Kansas we busted!" was a popular expression of the day.

Not all newcomers to America were Europeans whose route had taken them across the Atlantic to either settle on the East Coast or head west by rail. The railroads themselves, in fact, had been built to a large extent by immigrants from another far-distant land — China.

The first arrivals from across the Pacific made the long sea journey to California in the wake of the 1848 gold discovery. For the most part, they were men on their own rather than entire families. Perhaps *your* first ancestor in America was one of those desperately poor Chinese peasants longing to strike it rich in the gold fields. The peasants' dream was to return home with enough money to pay off their debts and free their families from the harsh demands of the wealthy landowners. Others sought to escape lives of grinding poverty in the crowded cities of Canton or Hong Kong.

Most of the early Chinese immigrants never made the hoped-for gold strike or the triumphant journey home. They settled for jobs as laborers and cooks in the gold-mining camps and lumbering camps, or as servants and farm workers in the homes and on the ranches of prosperous West Coast families. The Chinese were welcomed as cheap labor in the then-underpopulated West. Yet, almost from the start, they were poorly treated, both taken advantage of and despised because of their willingness to work for the lowest wages.

With the building of the Central Pacific Railroad, which was begun in the 1860s, more Chinese than ever were encouraged to come to America to work at backbreaking and dangerous jobs. As the rail line snaked eastward from Sacramento, California, its roadbed had to climb the slopes and descend the steep walls of the treacherous Sierra Nevada mountains. Many Chinese lost their lives bridging the swirling rivers, hacking tunnels through solid rock, and — in the final stages of building — toiling in the grueling heat of the Nevada desert.

At last, in 1869, the Central Pacific was linked with the Union Pacific, which had been constructed in a westerly direction from Omaha, Nebraska. The famous "Wedding of the Rails," at a meeting point in Utah, meant that the entire American continent could be crossed by train for the very first time.

But for the Chinese, whose "usefulness" was now over, the 1870s were a period of heightened and feverish racial persecution. Name-calling, robbings, beatings, even massacres took place all up and down the West Coast. Newspapers and politicians accused the Chinese of being "degraded," "inferior," and "without souls." But the real reason was that the Chinese now swelled the labor market and offered too much competition to white Americans seeking jobs. Other immigrant groups had been discriminated against as being "too different." And the potato-famine Irish had been looked down upon as living "no better than the pigs." But it was the Chinese who were singled out as the first foreign group to be denied further entry to the United States. An 1882 immigration law barring their admission was known as the Chinese Exclusion Act.

This unhappy comment on American democracy was repeated in the case of the Japanese, who began arriving in California in the 1890s. Racial prejudice sprang up afresh, although for a slightly different reason. While the Chinese "coolies" were so poor they were willing to work for depressed wages, the Japanese were considered too successful, especially as West Coast farmers. Worse, those who made up this new "yellow peril" were accused of being a secretive, spying people who threatened to overrun the

Japanese immigrants at the California receiving station of Angel Island in San Francisco Bay. Due to the fear of cholera, the station was also used as a quarantine center where newcomers might be held for weeks or months.

entire country. By 1907 the government of Japan was asked to sign a "Gentleman's Agreement" limiting exit visas for Japanese who wanted to emigrate to the United States. But, as the Japanese continued to prosper, more restrictions were called for. Yet another immigration law, the Oriental Exclusion Act, was passed in 1924, shutting the door to almost all Asians.

If you are of Japanese ancestry, the bitter chapter that followed may well be remembered by your grandparents. It began with Japan's surprise attack on Pearl Harbor in 1941, which triggered America's entry into World War II. At once, all the old suspicions of the Japanese came to the fore. Although no Japanese-American was ever found to be guilty of spying or sabotage, anti-Japanese feeling ran rampant. As a result, over one hundred thousand West Coast Japanese — most of them Nisei, or native-born Americans — were removed to internment camps for the duration of the war.

Those who were rounded up were given five days to leave their homes and businesses, taking only whatever they could carry. At the bleak and barren relocation centers, they were surrounded by barbed wire and military police. One Japanese-American later wrote of the scorching desert camp to which he was sent as "a place beyond description and beyond tears." Is there a sad memory of this kind in your family?

In more recent decades, the position of Asians, as well as many other minority groups in the United States, has changed for the better. But the internment of Japanese-Americans experienced by your grandparents' generation is an example of how the interplay of world events and a family's foreign heritage can affect the lives of its members.

❖

The Chinese and Japanese who immigrated to California to escape poverty and improve their opportunities were actually small in number compared with the massive influx of newcomers from Europe that was now taking place on the East Coast. Starting in the 1880s, steamships had begun to ply the Atlantic on regular and frequent schedules. The newer ships offered comfortable upper-deck staterooms for the wealthy as well as steerage class for the poor. The typically dark and airless steerage accommodations lay both fore and aft below decks. But some companies, like the White Star Line, which sailed out of Liverpool, England, to New York, made a point of advertising *its* steerage quarters as "unequalled for ventilation, light, and care for passengers' comfort."

The sleeping berths on most ships, however, consisted of bunks about three feet high, stacked up two or three to a tier. Privacy for family groups or for women traveling alone might be provided by little more than a blanket thrown over a line of rope. Toilet and bathing facilities were never adequate. And steerage passengers on all ships had to provide their own towels and bedding, as well as a plate, mug, knife, fork, spoon, and water can.

The White Star Line was proud to announce that it served steerage travelers soup and meat at one o'clock dinner, which was the main meal of the day, and pudding for dessert on Sunday. Most meals in steerage, though, consisted of bread, potatoes, porridge, and salted fish. The food was brought below decks in kettles and dished out. Water, however, usually had to be fetched in the passenger's own water can. As the ship could carry only a limited amount of fresh water, those in steerage were allowed just a few quarts a day for drinking and washing up.

Although the new steamships decreased the length of the journey to as little as ten days to two weeks, most voyages from ports in Germany, Italy, or Greece took closer to three weeks. Seasickness and other illnesses, discomfort and overcrowding, brought added misery with each day at sea. Fares ran about thirty dollars for adults and less for children. This was a lot of money for poor families, but none wanted a longer ocean voyage for the fare they paid. Interestingly, the transatlantic steamships of the 1880s were fitted with sails just in case their engines broke down!

A steamship company ad of the 1880s announcing details of its Atlantic crossings. Note that, although the ship pictured has two smokestacks, it is also outfitted with sails.

Where were all these people — your great-grandparents very possibly among them — coming from and why? The year 1907 saw more than 1.2 million newcomers enter the United States. What made it the peak immigration year in the country's entire history?

The answer can be traced almost directly to the swelling population, strangling poverty, and religious persecution then being suffered by millions of southern and eastern Europeans. America beckoned to them as it had to the mainly northern and western European emigrants of the 1800s. In southern Italy, for example, world prices for exports such as wheat, fruits, and wine had dropped sharply since the 1870s. The already low earnings of farm laborers shrank because farm products were worth less. Families living on as little as eight cents a day huddled with their livestock in straw huts and rock caves. Between 1880 and 1910, over three million Italians — both men on their own seeking work, and entire families — booked steerage passage to the United States.

Next largest in number — around two million — were Jews, mainly from Russia and eastern Poland, which had been under Russian domination for over one hundred years. Most Jews were forced to live in a part of western Russia known as the "pale of settlement," were prohibited from owning land, and were subject to long, harsh years of military service in the army of the Russian czar.

The single event that was to send countless Jewish families fleeing to America was the assassination in 1881 of Czar Alexander II by political terrorists. Although innocent of the crime, the Jews of Russia had long been singled out for blame in times of unrest. The rulers who followed Alexander made the lives of

Russia's Jews even more difficult than before. For the next thirty years, waves of beatings, burnings, lootings, and killings were directed against the Jews. Known as pogroms, these outbreaks were quietly approved by the Russian government as an outlet for the revolutionary anger of the country's frustrated masses.

Stories of Jews narrowly escaping across the Russian border beneath a wagonload of straw, especially if they were young men of draft age, were common. Jews who wanted to leave legally had to apply for passports. Often the hardest part, aside from leaving one's home and loved ones, was the journey across Europe to ports in Germany, Holland, or Belgium. Steamship-company agents generally arranged for crude lodgings en route and for places for the emigrants to stay in a port city while they were waiting for the ship to sail. But the travelers, who had to carry all their money and belongings with them, were often preyed upon by thieves and swindlers.

Jewish families had the special problem of bringing along enough provisions for the entire journey, by both land and sea, because their religion forbade the eating of non-kosher meats, fats, and other foods. A great-grandfather in his nineties, who arrived in America in 1904, recalls, "We carried with us dry black bread, so dry it couldn't turn moldy, and rendered beef fat. Once we were on board the ship, we soaked the bread and the fat in the boiling water that was used to make tea, and ate it like soup. We also ate the barreled herring they gave us. It was supposed to be good for seasickness. One of my brothers sneaked hot buns from the ship's kitchens. But we never told my parents because they were probably made with lard [hog fat] which of course wasn't kosher."

The third largest group of the peak immigration years, after the Italians and the Jews, were Poles, numbering about one million. In addition, there were Czechs and other Slavic peoples, Hungarians, Greeks, Portuguese, Armenians, and many more. As the long, hazardous journey drew to a close and the ship entered New York harbor, its steerage passengers crowded the decks for a first view of the "golden land." Those who arrived after 1886, the year the Statue of Liberty was erected, craned their necks to see the tall emblem of freedom. Some immigrants mistakenly believed it to be the tomb of Christopher Columbus.

A ship entering New York harbor in the near-peak immigration year of 1906, its steerage passengers massed on deck for a view of the new land

Although there were some seventy ports of entry for immigrants in the United States in the early 1900s, New York received 90 percent of the new arrivals. For those massed on deck, joy and relief were blended with fearful anticipation. Ahead lay the last hurdle, the receiving station where all foreigners in steerage had to be processed for admission into the country.

To prepare for landing, passengers dressed in their best clothes, often finding that they had lost weight from seasickness and poor food during the weeks at sea. They gathered their belongings—bedding, a pair of brass candlesticks, a child's favorite toy or doll. These scarce possessions were a mixture of treasured reminders of their homeland and the necessities of everyday living. All the while, the passengers' minds seethed with worries. Would they be able to give satisfactory answers to the immigration officials? There would be questions about their name, age, place of origin, marital status, job skills, and how much money they carried with them. For women traveling alone, would the promised relative, fiancé, or other responsible party be there to meet them? Worst of all, would a family be threatened with separation because one member—a child, perhaps—failed to pass the dreaded medical examination?

❖

"It was a regular Castle Garden!" Have you ever heard this expression used by some older person in your family? What that person is describing is a scene of almost unimaginable confusion, crowding, and noise. For this is the way New York City's first immigrant receiving station, opened in 1855, appeared to most new arrivals.

By 1892 Castle Garden, originally built as a fort off the lower tip of Manhattan Island and later connected to it by landfill, had become so overcrowded that it had to be replaced. The new and much larger facility was laid out on Ellis Island, about a mile offshore in New York harbor. But here, too, the scene was so baffling that for many years to come immigrants were to insist on referring to it as "Castle Garden."

The main building on Ellis Island was the biggest that most immigrants had ever seen. It contained a huge two-story hall with baggage rooms, waiting rooms, and examination areas. It had dormitories, dining halls, and hospital wards for those who were detained on the island. It even had a postal and telegraph office, a bank for changing money, and a railroad-ticketing office.

Almost everyone who ever passed through Ellis Island remembers something of the strangeness and the embarrassments that confronted them there. "My father, who had come to America before us," one woman recalls from her childhood, "met us at Ellis Island and handed me a banana. I'd never seen one before. I bit into it skin and all. I didn't even know you had to peel it!"

Another immigrant who came over as a young man told how he had always believed that America was a warm country because he had seen pictures of bare-chested American Indians in headdresses and loincloths. So he sold his overcoat before leaving his home town in Europe to help pay for his sea passage. "I arrived at Ellis Island in early winter," he admitted sheepishly, "and nearly froze to death."

One thirteen-year-old girl who was traveling alone with the address of an American relative crumpled up in her hand felt so homesick and frightened that she cried for days aboard the ship. "Better not cry anymore," a fellow passenger warned her as they awaited the transfer barge that would take them from the steam-

Tagging a German immigrant family for a railway journey westward, a function of the railroad-ticketing office at busy Ellis Island

ship to Ellis Island, "or your eyes will be so red the doctors will think you have trachoma."

Trachoma, a contagious eye disease that can lead to blindness, was one of the main reasons for an immigrant's being sent back to Europe on the next available ship. Almost as feared as the doctor's verdict was the examination itself. Some immigrants insisted that their eyelids had been painfully rolled back with a buttonhook, the same kind that was used for fastening the rows of buttons on the gloves people wore at that time.

Another disease that could mean deportation was favus, a contagious scalp condition caused by a fungus. Medical examiners also inspected the newcomers for signs of tuberculosis, heart trouble, hernia, lameness, deafness, epilepsy, mental re-

Being checked for trachoma, a serious eye disease, by an Ellis Island medical examiner

tardation, and other ills that might prevent the new arrivals from earning a living and turn them into public charges.

The number of would-be immigrants who were refused entry at Ellis Island between 1892 and 1920 averaged about two out of every one hundred, or 2 percent. This doesn't sound like a lot until we remember that twelve million people were processed on the island in that period. This meant that the actual number of returnees was about 240,000. The rejected immigrants had no money for their sea passage, so the steamship companies were required to carry them free of charge. As time passed, the shipping companies became increasingly strict about inspecting steerage travelers for health problems *before* they embarked for America.

The final step for the newcomers — most of whom successfully passed through Ellis Island in a single, although harrowing, day — was the short ferry ride from the island receiving station to Manhattan. Many were to remain in New York City, swelling its immigrant population to about 75 percent of its total inhabitants by the year 1910. Others were to head overland to more distant destinations by railroad or other means of transportation.

As the ferry docked in Lower Manhattan, almost all the new arrivals were taken aback by the bustle and noise, the elevated trains and clanging trolley cars, the sheer density of people thronging the city's streets. This was yet another memorable moment for a newcomer, one that was almost certain to remain

Cleared at last by the officials on Ellis Island, an immigrant group waits with its baggage for the ferry that will take it to Manhattan and the start of a new life.

so for a lifetime. Can you find a story describing the first impression *your* immigrant ancestor had of the land in which you and your family live today?

❖

On the other hand, perhaps you yourself have a "first impression" to report. For, although immigration declined after 1921 (and Ellis Island itself was closed in 1954), a rising number of "new" immigrants are today arriving in the United States. If you are among them, you may find that in years to come *you* will be the "immigrant ancestor" whom future generations will look to.

Between the 1920s and the 1960s, the United States government kept a fairly tight lid on immigration. The aftermath of World War I, the Great Depression of the 1930s, and World War II in the 1940s created much anti-foreign sentiment. But, since the mid-1960s, the door has opened wider. The new immigrants are coming for reasons that are not much different from those of the "old" immigrants of the early 1900s. They are seeking to escape from religious persecution, political oppression, poverty, and homelessness. Above all, they are searching for freedom and for educational and economic opportunity. They now arrive mainly by air rather than by sea. And they include a very large proportion — about 80 percent — of Asians and Latin Americans. Among them, too, are Soviet Jews, other Europeans, and smaller numbers from Africa and the Middle East.

Many of the new immigrants have been admitted as refugees, people who cannot safely return to the country from which they have come for fear of serious reprisals. Others are admitted to be reunited with family members who are already here. And still

New immigrants, a high proportion of whom are from Latin America, are drawn to the United States for reasons similar to those of the "old" immigrants—an escape from poverty, a chance for betterment.

others are welcomed because of special job or professional skills that are in demand in the United States.

Coming to live in the United States from Korea or the Philippines, Santo Domingo or Haiti is a dramatic chapter in the life of a family. Young people, especially, may be all too ready to discard the past and to forget the heritage they have left behind.

While many new immigrants in their pre-teens and teens have told how threatened they felt at first by the language barrier, the schools, and the challenges of finding their way around on big-city subway systems, most have quickly adapted to their new life. Asked if they would ever want to go back to their country of birth if they could, the majority of students in a New York City junior high school said no. Answers ranged from the thoughtful statement "Here we have more choices for our future" to the youthfully frivolous "Except for Bangkok [the capital], there's better action here than in Thailand!"

Not wishing to return to a way of life that has become distasteful for any of a variety of reasons is understandable. But we also need to remember that a family's history doesn't begin with its arrival in the United States. We are each the product of long-term cultural influences, as well as a long line of people.

The very richness of American life lies in the fact that the United States is not a "melting pot" in which everyone has merged into a featureless, gray mass. Rather, it is a mosaic, made up of people from numerous cultures who take pride and pleasure in their origins. That, after all, is what our individual family stories are all about.

The design of a great-great-grandmother's embroidered sampler, treasured by her family for four generations

FOUR

Family Treasures, Family Pleasures

*A*n old wedding dress with a veil of yellowing lace, a pair of baby shoes of crinkled white leather, a first-grade report card, a handmade Valentine, a dried and faded flower from a corsage worn to a high school prom. . . . Are there possessions like these tucked away in a drawer, a closet, an attic storeroom in your home, or that of a close relative? Often such bits of personal and family memorabilia are tattered and brittle. They may be of no value to the outside world. Yet, among all the items that pass through our hands day after day, somebody chose to save these particular ones.

The places that these keepsakes have been, the people who have seen or handled them, the feelings they have evoked are all part of the story they tell. For four generations, one family has kept and displayed a framed needlework sampler. Its center is embroidered in many-colored threads with a pattern of a peacock surrounded by leaves and flowers. At the top of the embroidery are the initials *S.K.* and, at the bottom, the date *1895*, all worked in cross-stitch.

Samplers similar to this one began to be made as early as the 1500s. Young girls and women embroidered the letters of the alphabet, numbers, verses, sayings, and pictures on cloth to show examples — or "samples" — of their skill with various needlework stitches. Sometimes they added their initials, their age, or the date, making a sampler a meaningful family "document" as well as a family treasure.

Who was the S.K. whose handiwork was passed on from one generation to the next? Where was she in 1895, and what thoughts did she have as she sat with her embroidery before her? Her story is one of loneliness and fear of abandonment. But it is also one that has a happy ending.

At the time she made her sampler, S.K. was a young married woman with an infant daughter. She was living in a poor village in northwestern Russia. Six months earlier, her young husband, due to be taken into the czar's army, which was notorious for its harsh treatment of Jews, had left Russia in the dark of night. Now he was in America, rooming with strangers in a tenement flat and trying to find steady work as a tailor. He was living on bakery rolls and coffee for pennies a day in order to save enough money to bring his wife and baby over from Europe.

Young emigrant men such as he were sometimes known to vanish into the crowded cities across the sea, never to be heard from again. Others took many years to send for their families. Often husbands and wives were strangers when at last they met once more. Would S.K., who was herself an orphan, be left to the uncertainties and dangers of Jewish life in czarist Russia? The fact that this great-great-grandmother's embroidered sampler has been in America for close to a century tells us that she *was* reunited with her husband and lived out her life here after all.

In another family, there may not be a sampler that tells a story. But there may be an old pieced-together quilt that crossed the plains, bits of handmade lace, a knitted or crocheted shawl or afghan from a beloved grandmother. There may be keepsakes such as ringlets of baby hair, souvenirs in the form of old ticket stubs and theater programs, "found" objects like a collection of seashells or rock samples from a memorable outing or vacation. There may be medals, awards, or trophies recalling honors bestowed in days gone by. Often, too, there are family heirlooms — a gold locket, a crystal vase, a pair of silver candlesticks.

What would any of these articles say if they could speak to us? Unlocking the secrets within these "treasures" may be as simple as asking questions of older relatives about them. By combining the answers with your other family-history notes, you will be enriching and illuminating *your* family's heritage. You will also have made a valuable record for generations to come.

Among other treasures that families hold onto are those made of paper. They range from family bibles to old diaries, letters, and scrapbooks; from baby-record books to high-school autograph albums; from birth announcements to college diplomas; from wedding invitations to death certificates.

An old family bible can be especially useful in providing clues for ancestor hunters. Starting in the late 1700s, it became the custom for young couples to receive bibles as wedding gifts. On the blank first page or pages, they recorded their marriage, the births of their children, and other family events such as baptisms, confirmations, and deaths. As it traveled through the years and accumulated more information, the bible grew into an outline of the family's history.

Other paper treasures tell us of the pride our immigrant ancestors took in acquiring official documents with their names on them. To be the owner of a passport, of "working papers," and especially of "citizenship papers" was a mark of having become "somebody," of establishing an identity for oneself in the new land.

Back in the early 1900s, for example, many immigrants entered the United States with forged or borrowed passports. Valid passports were often difficult to obtain and cost money that poor families could ill afford.

A proper passport, however, gave one permission to leave one's country of birth legally and to travel through other countries under the protection of the home country. So an immigrant who arrived in America with a government-issued passport from Russia, Italy, Greece, or some other foreign nation was especially proud to be starting out with a genuine passport in hand. No wonder such documents were carefully preserved in families long after their usefulness had ended.

A next step in an immigrant family might be for one of the children to apply for "working papers." In New York City in the early 1900s, young people were allowed to leave school and look for a full-time job at fourteen. Education was important, but so was the need to help out with the family's income and also have a little pocket money of one's own. So, many youngsters never went on to high school. With a grade-school education, they trudged the city's streets seeking almost any kind of work in a

A passport, costing fifteen rubles, issued in Grodno, Russia, on April 15, 1904. The page at the left gives the names of the traveling party, a mother and her four children aged five to fifteen years. The photograph shows one of the children who had traveled on the passport as he appeared ten years later.

factory, store, or warehouse to start them on the road to earning a living. The bright yellow Employment Certificate from the Board of Health was an immigrant teenager's ticket of admission to adulthood and independence.

Even more eventful than a first job was the day on which an immigrant became a citizen of the United States. By going through the process known as "naturalization," a foreigner could be granted the same rights of citizenship as a "natural-born" American. The applicant had to meet several requirements. One of the necessary steps for an immigrant was to have lived in the United States continuously for five years.

It was, and still is, the dream of most immigrants to one day take the oath of loyalty to their adopted country and to share in the rights and privileges that country offers its people. Among the valued documents in your family's collection, there is very likely to be a relative's certificate of naturalization, popularly known as "citizenship papers."

❖

A family's memories of itself are made up of much more, of course, than old documents and pieces of antique needlework. Meaningful as those memorabilia may be, they don't tell the whole story. For family history is also living history — and even history in the making.

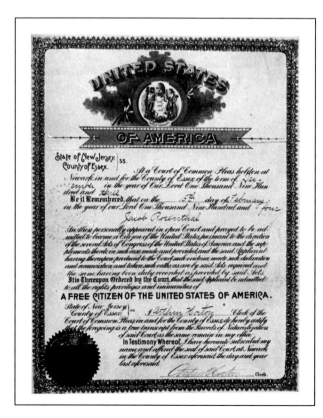

This citizenship certificate, dated 1904 and issued by a local court in the state of New Jersey, was the proud possession of a great-great-grandfather who immigrated to the United States in the 1890s.

The next time your family gets together for a holiday dinner, a birthday party, or some other special occasion, listen carefully for the shared expressions, jokes, songs, and stories that make your family unique, different in character from all other families.

Does somebody *always* tell about the time fussy old Great-Uncle Horace took five little nieces and nephews on an ice cream outing and was so fearful they would misbehave that he suggested they be given "spankings in advance"? Is father *always* reminded of the time he was three years old and called grandpa's pompous Cousin Jacques "dummyhead"? Sent to his room as a punishment, he later voiced his innocence with the excuse "I just didn't know his name."

Every family has its recipes, its eating traditions, and its occasional food and cooking disasters to recall. There was the time the spaghetti sauce was left on the stove too long and was burnt black, the time the party sandwiches were stolen from the church basement by neighborhood mischief-makers, the time the dog ate the anniversary cake.

There are the wonderful-tasting dishes to remember, like grandma's feather-light dumplings with chicken stew. And the not-so-great ones, like Great-Aunt Sophie's deviled-tongue croquettes. And there are the special holiday food traditions that the family has always observed, like having a velvety egg-and-lemon soup on Easter Eve or a turkey stuffed with pecans and cornbread on Thanksgiving.

All of these customs and remembrances make up what we call our family's folklore. In the very act of laughing, sighing, or nodding over the shared experiences that bind us, we are not just reliving the past. We are also reinventing it. We are creating new folkloric experiences that will be recalled with pleasure at future family get-togethers.

Unlike the dates, places, and other hard facts we look for in filling in a family-history chart, the subject matter of family folklore doesn't have to be fixed or exact. Each time a story is told, it may be changed a little by the teller, who brings something of himself or herself to it. Family folklore lives and grows. Some old tales inevitably fade away, and new stories, or new versions of old stories, are woven into this informal collection.

Family get-togethers are also a wonderful time for asking our relatives what their lives were like when they were our age. What were the clothes and hair styles of the day? What music did they enjoy? What were their favorite toys, games, pastimes, and hobbies? How did they spend their summer vacations? How were things different from today?

A grandmother tells about growing up in the years before World War II, when there was no TV, there were no plastics, and—worst of all—no antibiotics or polio vaccines. The polio epidemic of the 1930s, she recalls, was an especially scary time. Everyone was terrified of catching the disease. So she and her family spent summers at a country hotel, far away from the crowds of the city. And she shows a picture of a children's masquerade party taken at that hotel, with adult guests looking on from the balcony above. It's hard to imagine your grandmother at six, in a crepe-paper dress and a big hair bow. But there she is.

Does your grandfather have a favorite story about when he was a young man? Perhaps he has described to you his "secret" sailing to Europe on a giant troop carrier during World War II. Nobody was allowed to know when one of the faster ships, its

Your grandmother in the crepe-paper costume she wore to a children's masquerade party that took place at a country hotel one summer long ago

portholes blackened, set out across the Atlantic without an escort, hoping to outrun the German submarines. As the wartime posters read, "Loose lips sink ships!" Can you picture your grandfather at eighteen going to war aboard that ship—one of fifteen thousand men in enough space for half that number, sleeping in eight-hour rotation shifts and washing up in heated salt water?

Or does your grandparent have an experience to relate of life during the Holocaust, the Nazi annihilation of six million Jews? How did he or she avoid dying in the gas chambers of the German concentration camps, as did other family members? Jewish children were sometimes hidden by brave and kindly people, or were sent away to safety in countries not under Nazi domination. But many actually spent time in concentration camps and weren't liberated until World War II ended in Europe.

Stories of narrow escapes in wartime, of heroic acts of rescue, of natural disasters like floods and tornados, of tragically lost opportunities all make up the drama of our families' rememberings.

Happily, there are also the less serious tales that are recalled over and over again. They may be about the romantic twists and turns of a courtship; about how a great fortune was *almost* made by some enterprising relative; or about an old family superstition or a supernatural happening that is sworn to be true. And there are the lighthearted, even giddy, reminiscences of the pranks and practical jokes played on or by family members.

Lastly, almost all families have a collection of special words and phrases that are part of their folklore. Some are expressions that have been handed down by older relatives. Others come directly out of the mispronounced words of young children.

We can't help laughing as we learn that our father "talked funny" when he was little and said things like "pizghetti," for spaghetti, until he was seven years old. Or that our mother used to say "chicken pops" for chicken pox and, for quite a long time, thought they were something good to eat.

What about our own baby words? We all love to hear stories about "when we were little," and they, too, become part of our

Was this really your father when he was three, wearing a cowboy hat and riding on a rubber duck?

family's folklore. Which of us didn't have a favorite "blankie" or a tattered "teddy" that had to be sneaked into the wash? What was the special song, story, or "good-night" ritual that could always be counted on to put us to sleep? What can we learn, through the rememberings of our families, about a time that is hidden from us behind the haze of babyhood?

❖

Was your mother once this wide-eyed baby whose first words are still recalled by her mother—and who in turn will pass on to you her rememberings of your babyhood?

As the search for our roots—both our family's and our own—goes on, we probably will find that we are building up quite a collection of material. Is there some ideal way of "getting it all together" in a form that is also going to be convenient for "passing it on"?

The choice of how to preserve our personal time-lines, direct-ancestry charts, family-interview notes, and much more is really our own. Some of us may prefer a looseleaf notebook or a folder in which to keep our findings. Others may choose to make up a scrapbook with accompanying photographs. We may also have old home movies, tape recordings, and even videotapes that bring our family's history and folklore together, as well as the writings, documents, and keepsakes of our ancestors. So a large, sturdy box or even a small chest may be the answer.

It's a good idea, too, to photocopy all written and printed materials in case the originals are lost. And old family pictures can be photographed, giving us new photos and a set of negatives as well.

One of the great pleasures of being the family "historian" is that of sharing what you've learned. You can do this by starting a family club, circulating a family newsletter, or helping to arrange a family reunion. It's not at all unlikely that your efforts will be rewarded by finding relatives who have also been working on your family's story and who can add to what you already know.

In some unforeseen way, working on your heritage may even lead you into a career choice you otherwise might not have dreamed of. Getting "hooked" on family history and family-story material could result in your becoming a genealogist specializing in tracing family lines for individuals or for medical or legal personnel; a library or museum archivist working with public records and historical documents; a researcher of the oral history traditions of various world cultures; a biographer, journalist, photographer, or documentary film-maker.

But even if *all* that happens as a result of your ancestor hunt is that your "sense of family" is awakened and broadened, you will have become richer for the experience.

Your hope of proving that your family owns an authentic coat of arms—an insignia worn in the tournaments and Crusades of the Middle Ages—probably will be dashed. The same may be true of your dream of finding yourself related to an American

"Collecting" our ancestors and "talking family" are among the rewards of hunting for our roots.

president or a superstar of the entertainment world. You may have failed to discover your grandmother's maiden name *or* her secret remedy for curing everything from hiccups to hives. You may not even have been able to find out where in Africa, Asia, Latin America, or Europe your family originally lived.

In fact, the main achievement of your family-roots research may be your *own* life story, told in a time-line, notebook, photo scrapbook, diary, or other personal-history format. The value of recording what you've learned about yourself and those who are part of your everyday life is considerable. In finding out who you are, you are putting together an offering that will strengthen the ties between the present and the future.

Above all, what you've been doing in hunting ancestors is "talking family." In drawing together with those who are closest to you, you have brightened *your* family's "moment" in human history with caring and love.

❖ ◆◆◆ APPENDIX ◆◆◆ ❖

Digging Deeper:

PUBLIC RECORDS THAT MAY HELP
IN YOUR ANCESTOR HUNT

Today we live in an age of information. Computers can provide instant and accurate facts about numerous aspects of our lives. In the not-so-distant past, record keeping was very different. And back in 1790, when the first United States census was taken, no questionnaires or even blank sheets of paper were given to the door-to-door census takers. Some records were actually written down, often in semi-legible penmanship, on strips of wallpaper!

Unlike modern-day records, information was seldom cross-checked. Errors arose from both those who provided the facts and those who entered them. And further mistakes were made when records were hand-copied or otherwise transcribed.

However, for ancestor hunters who would like to probe deeper into the past, there are a number of official and other public sources that may prove of interest. Serious detective work can turn up some thrilling discoveries such as an ancestor's name on a forgotten gravestone, on a ship's passenger list, even perhaps on a military record from the American Revolution.

Census Records: Genealogists consider the United States federal census records one of the best places to start when seeking official information about our ancestors. Prior to the federal censuses, begun in 1790 and taken every ten years thereafter, the colonies conducted censuses from time to time. Some colonial records from roughly 1600 to 1789 survive, but they are scattered and incomplete.

As described earlier, the federal censuses of 1790 through 1840 listed only heads of households by name. These included "free white" men and women, "free blacks," and a very few American Indians. For those of us who may have had a black ancestor then living in a non-slave state, there is a special *List of Free Black Heads of Families in the First Census of the United States, 1790*. It is available from the National Archives (address given below).

The 1790 census records are limited, of course, to the states (the former thirteen colonies) that then made up the Union, and to their adjoining territories. Kentucky was part of Virginia at the time, and Tennessee was part of North Carolina. Vermont, although not admitted to the Union until 1791, was also included in the 1790 census.

Even so, there are gaps. The records for Maryland and North Carolina do not cover all counties. And those of Delaware, Georgia, Kentucky, New Jersey, Tennessee, and Virginia were largely destroyed when the British set fire to the Capitol in Washington, D.C., during the War of 1812.

The 1850 census was the first to list all household members by name and to give the exact age, occupation, and place of birth of each. Slaves, however, were not individually identified. From 1790 through 1860, they were simply entered as to number under the name of the slave owner. It wasn't until the 1870 census —

the first one taken after the Civil War—that all black Americans began to be listed by name.

Special censuses of American Indians of the Creek and Cherokee Nations were conducted in 1832 and 1835, respectively. But Indians did not really begin to be counted until the 1860 census, which focused on those living among the general population. For Indians living on reservations, the federal government undertook special yearly censuses for most years from 1885 to 1940.

The 1880 regular federal census provided additional information of value to ancestor hunters. It asked for the relationship of each member of the household to the head of the family and also the place of birth of each person's parents. Added to the 1890, 1900, and 1910 censuses were questions directed at immigrants, asking when they had arrived in the United States, whether they spoke English, and whether they had become naturalized citizens.

Unfortunately, almost all of the 1890 census was destroyed by fire in 1921. It's helpful to know that a number of states conducted censuses of their own during the 1800s and early 1900s. New York State, for example, took a census every ten years from 1825 to 1925. Information can be obtained from the local offices of the county clerk throughout the state. Addresses and phone numbers are listed in most telephone directories.

What about the federal censuses of 1920 and thereafter? It's the government's policy not to release census information to the general public until seventy-two years have elapsed. However, specific requests about oneself, about a close relative, or from a legal heir are usually honored.

Questions about obtaining federal census information that is open to the general public may be directed to:

> National Archives and Records Administration
> Washington, D.C. 20408

In addition, there are eleven regional branches of the National Archives located around the country. The address and telephone number of the branch nearest you can be found under the *United States Government* listings in your local telephone directory, or by calling the *Federal Information Center* number under that listing. Microfilms of federal census records for a particular locality or region can also be found in many of the larger public libraries in that area.

For information about census records that are less than seventy-two years old, request an *Application for Search of Census Records* from:

> Bureau of the Census
> United States Department of Commerce
> Pittsburg, Kansas 66762

One of the things to remember about looking up census records is that the counts were done geographically, by state. Each state was divided into counties. Cities were further divided into special districts called wards. So it is helpful to know three things: the census year you want to investigate; the address at which your ancestor was living at the time; and the surname of your ancestor.

If you know the city but not the address, you may be able to find it in something called a city directory, which is a little like a telephone directory from before the age of the telephone. Many cities in the eastern half of the country published such directories yearly during the 1800s. They listed each inhabitant by name and also gave that person's address and occupation. Once you know the exact address, a historic city map can guide you to the ward. For an ancestor who lived out in the country, a regional map of the period showing the counties with the names of the landowners in each of them may be helpful in guiding you to the specific county. City directories and old city and county maps are often available for reference at regional public libraries or historical societies.

If you don't have sufficiently detailed information about where your ancestor lived, your search won't be entirely hopeless, but it will take much longer. Being able to look up your ancestor by name rather than address is generally a lot easier. And, fortunately, some censuses have been indexed so that, provided you know the state, you can search by surname.

Suppose, however, you have the wrong spelling. Many family names were misspelled in the records or were spelled differently from today. To broaden your chances of finding your ancestor in the census, a code known as the Soundex system was used for indexing the entire 1900 census and parts of the 1880 and 1910 censuses.

Here's how the Soundex system works. All consonants with the exception of *H*, *W*, and *Y* are assigned a number as follows:

Code Number	Letter(s) in Number Group
1	B, F, P, V
2	C, G, J, K, Q, S, X, Z
3	D, T
4	L
5	M, N
6	R

The Soundex coding of a family name is made up of an initial, which is the first letter of the name, and three numbers. To find the Soundex "spelling" beyond the initial, all vowels (*A, E, I, O,* and *U*) and the letters *H, W,* and *Y* are omitted from the name. Double consonants are treated as one letter. And two or more adjoining consonant sounds that fall into the same number group, as in a name like Be*ck*er, are treated as one.

As an example, the name *Reynolds* would be identified as R543 (R = first initial; 5 = N; 4 = L; 3 = D). Suppose your ancestor or the census taker spelled the family name *Raynolds, Renholds, Reinhold, Reinold,* or *Rynold.* The Soundex code name would still be the same. And, by then looking for the first name under the code listing, you'd be less likely to miss out on the person you were seeking. Of course, in the case of many Soundex surnames with the same first names, you'd also have to know a spouse's first name, a date of birth, or some other identifying fact to help you pin down the correct person.

In the Soundex system, surnames with fewer than three consonant sounds after the initial end in one or more zeros. For example, a name like *Brown* (also possibly spelled *Browne, Broun, Broune, Braun, Bronn,* or *Bron,* among others) is coded as B650. *Keen,* as well as *Keene, Kean, Keane, Keehan, Kehan,* and several more spellings, would be K500. And a name with no consonant sounds after the initial, like *Lee, Lea,* or *Li,* would be L000.

Digging for your family roots in the federal census records may seem like rather hard work. But, depending on which census year you investigate, you can come up with clues to all sorts of other information.

Learning an exact address, for example, can guide you to the school your ancestor went to or the local church or synagogue where the family worshipped. From these sources, you may unearth further material. Most census records tell about property ownership and can lead to your finding land deeds, mortgages, and even wills through local sources. Military service was reported in a number of census years and can be checked further in state archives or, starting with the American Revolution, in the National Archives. And even approximate dates and places of births, marriages, and deaths taken from census records can give you enough facts to write away for the official papers that registered these events.

Vital Records: This is the name given to records of births, marriages, and deaths that have been registered by state and local government agencies. Unlike the United States census records, however, almost none go as far back as 1790. In fact, fewer than a dozen states began to officially register births and deaths much before the early 1900s. Before that time, records were kept by scattered towns and counties, or by religious institutions, and are understandably much harder to trace.

Because they are a sort of summing up, death certificates usually give more information about an ancestor than do birth or marriage certificates. Not only do we learn the date, place, and cause of death. The date and place of birth, marital status, occupation, place of residence, name of attending physician, name of undertaker, and place of burial also usually appear. Even the names, and possibly the birthplaces, of the parents of the deceased may be on the certificate.

Just like census records, vital records—official as they may look—often contain errors. But they can also be quite accurate and can point the way to further discoveries. Among them might be an obituary in a local newspaper, tracked down from the date on a death certificate. In an obituary, we often find the names of family members of the deceased, as well as any professional, social, religious, or patriotic organizations to which our ancestor belonged. Other useful facts may also be included in the newspaper account. And, of course, knowing a relative's place of burial can lead you, via cemetery records, to the grave itself.

Serious ancestor hunters often make a hobby of "collecting" gravestone inscriptions. Frequently, the stone carvings fill in all sorts of information gaps, such as the deceased's birthplace, precise age, spouse's name, and names of parents or children. Older gravestones can be particularly interesting in design. And often one grave marker leads to another, as additional family members are found to be buried nearby.

The best ways to "collect" family gravestones are through photographs or rubbings. Older stones may have to be gently cleaned first so that there will be a sharp contrast between the surface and the inscription. Rubbings are done by fastening a large sheet of thin, good-quality white paper to the face of the stone with masking tape. When the paper is rubbed carefully with the side of a large crayon or colored wax cake, the engraved areas that make up the inscription will show up in white.

Even in cases where grave markers have never been erected or have crumbled, sunken, or otherwise disappeared, cemetery records can often supply important facts. Among them may even be the name of a living descendant of the deceased. Also, some of our ancestors—especially those of the immigrant period of the early 1900s—may have purchased their burial plots through a lodge, club, or other benevolent or mutual-aid society. Here is another lead turned up through a cemetery record. The lodge or club historian may have much to tell us about our forebear who was once a member.

Vital records, also known as vital statistics in some states, are undeniably useful. These certificates of birth, marriage, and death are generally available from offices in the state capitals. Or they may be obtained at the local level from county, town, or city departments. The telephone directory or the local library can almost always guide you to where to write for them. Or you can send for a pamphlet put out by the United States Department of Health and Human services called *Where to Write for Vital Records*. The address is:

> Consumer Information Center—Z
> P.O. Box 100
> Pueblo, Colorado 81002

Immigration and Naturalization Records: One of the more promising ways to check for records of our ancestors' immigration into the United States is through passenger lists of the ships they sailed on. The *Mayflower* is an excellent example of a ship with a well-preserved passenger list. In fact, the names of those who made the voyage from England to the New World in the year 1620 have become part of history.

Unfortunately, records of most sailings to America that took place before the year 1820 are spotty, and sources are widely scattered. From 1820 on, however, federal law required that, on arrival at a United States port, the ship's captain was to file a passenger list with port officials. It was to contain the name, age, sex, occupation, country of origin, and other information about each passenger on board.

Although there are many gaps, especially for West Coast ports, ships' passenger lists from 1820 to 1945 are now obtainable from the National Archives. It's exciting indeed to find the name of an immigrant ancestor on a ship's passenger list. It's important to remember, though, that the lists are arranged by port of arrival (New York, Baltimore, Boston, Philadelphia, etc.). Also, in addition to knowing the port, one should know the name of the ship and the date of arrival.

Our ancestors' naturalization records — their "citizenship papers" — may also require more information than we have at hand, especially if the certificates were issued before 1906. Although Congress passed a naturalization law way back in 1790, local courts in the various states were empowered to grant citizenship. As in the case of other non-centralized records, they are scattered around the country, and one would have to know where one's ancestor was living at the time of application. However, a *few* pre-1906 records, mainly for certain New England states, can be found in the National Archives.

In 1906 a federal agency called the Bureau of Immigration and Naturalization was established in Washington, D.C., and a standard three-step procedure for naturalization was instituted. It consisted of a Declaration of Intent, known as "first papers," a Final Petition, and at last the Certificate of Naturalization itself. Local courts were required to file all documents with the new federal bureau. Some immigrants, of course, never became citizens. And children who were born in the United States were citizens automatically, so no naturalization papers would have been filed. Also, between 1855 and 1922, a woman could become a citizen simply by marrying a man who had either been born in the United States or been naturalized. This law was changed in 1922 to avoid "marriage mills" — a practice whereby an alien would marry an American purely to gain citizenship.

In seeking our ancestors' naturalization records, we must also remember that the original citizenship laws applied only to "free whites." Black Americans, including those born on American soil, were not granted citizenship until 1868. (And, shockingly, not all American Indians attained this right until 1924!)

The Declaration of Intent, or so-called first papers, required of an applicant for naturalization often carried broad background information of much interest and value to ancestor hunters. To find out about obtaining naturalization records starting with September 26, 1906, write to:

Immigration and Naturalization Service
425 Eye Street, N.W.
Washington, D.C. 20536

Records of the Genealogical Society of Utah: The Genealogical Society of Utah is a branch of the Church of Jesus Christ of Latter-day Saints, widely known as the Mormon church. Many privately funded genealogical research groups exist, both in the United States and abroad. The Mormons' undertaking, however, is said to contain the largest collection of genealogical records in the world—the names of over 1.5 billion people who have lived since the 1500s.

Further, the Mormon group estimates that information may be available for as many as six or seven billion people who were born after 1500 or so. This is when records for ordinary people began to be kept. Before that time, only the family lines of rich and powerful persons are believed to be traceable.

The Genealogical Society of Utah's interest in microfilming centuries-old records from as many countries of the world as possible stems in part from its related religious beliefs. The Church of Jesus Christ of Latter-day Saints was founded in the United States in 1830, making it one of the world's newer faiths. Accordingly, church members are encouraged to trace their family lines back for four generations or more so that even long-deceased relatives can be inducted into the church through a proxy ceremony. But the Genealogical Society's files also go well beyond the names of ancestors of church members.

Indexed records of births, baptisms, marriages, deaths, land deeds, wills, and many other key materials, often taken from hard-to-find foreign sources, are available to the general public. As with many public records, more recent information is restricted for a certain time period to protect the privacy of the subject and next of kin.

As foreign-born ancestors are seldom easy to trace prior to their arrival in the United States, it may be well worth finding out if they have been documented by the Genealogical Society of Utah. A great deal of research has been done on immigrants from western and northern Europe. On the other hand, a number of foreign countries either have little in the way of records or have been reluctant to share them with the Genealogical Society's researchers. Still, new material is steadily being gathered.

The Genealogical Society of Utah has hundreds of branch libraries all over the United States and in foreign countries as well. To find the name of the branch nearest you, look in your local telephone directory under Church of Jesus Christ of Latter-day Saints, or write to:

Genealogical Society of Utah
50 East North Temple Street
Salt Lake City, Utah 84150

In reading about how to hunt for official and other public records, it may often seem that we need to start by knowing almost as much about our ancestors as we're trying to find out. To a certain extent, this is true. The more information we can gather from family interviews, the more clues we will have when it comes to digging into census reports, vital records, and the like.

The greater challenge, of course, is to try to work with just a few main clues that will, in time, dramatically unlock many mysteries of the past. Whether we choose to use living sources only or to probe the public-record files as well, the main thing to remember is to view our "great ancestor hunt" as an enjoyable and enriching adventure.

❖ ➤➤➤ BIBLIOGRAPHY ◄◄◄ ❖

BENTON, BARBARA. *Ellis Island: A Pictorial History.* New York: Facts on File, 1985.

BROWNSTONE, DAVID M., IRENE M. FRANCK, and DOUGLASS L. BROWNSTONE. *Island of Hope, Island of Tears.* New York: Rawson, Wade Publishers, 1979.

CAREY, HELEN H., and JUDITH E. GREENBERG. *How to Use Primary Sources.* New York: Franklin Watts, 1983.

CRANDALL, RALPH. *Shaking Your Family Tree: A Basic Guide to Tracing Your Family's Genealogy.* Dublin, N.H.: Yankee Publishing, 1986.

DINNERSTEIN, LEONARD, and DAVID M. REIMERS. *Ethnic Americans: A History of Immigration and Assimilation.* New York: Dodd, Mead, 1975.

DOANE, GILBERT H., and JAMES B. BELL. *Searching for Your Ancestors: The How and Why of Genealogy.* 5th ed. Minneapolis: University of Minnesota Press, 1980.

EPSTEIN, ELLEN ROBINSON, and RONA MENDELSOHN. *Record and Remember: Tracing Your Roots through Oral History.* New York: Sovereign Books, Simon and Schuster, 1978.

FLETCHER, WILLIAM. *Recording Your Family History*. New York: Dodd, Mead, 1986.

HALEY, ALEX. *Roots: The Saga of an American Family*. New York: Doubleday, 1976.

HELMBOLD, F. WILBUR. *Tracing Your Ancestry: A Step-by-Step Guide to Researching Your Family History*. Birmingham, Ala.: Oxmoor House, 1976.

KRANZLER, DAVID. *My Jewish Roots: A Practical Guide to Tracing and Recording Your Genealogy and Family History*. New York: Sepher-Hermon Press, 1979.

LICHTMAN, ALLAN J. *Your Family History*. New York: Vintage/Random House, 1978.

LINDER, BILL R. *How to Trace Your Family History*. New York: Everest House, 1978.

ROTTENBERG, DAN. *Finding Our Fathers: A Guidebook to Jewish Genealogy*. New York: Random House, 1977.

SHOUMATOFF, ALEX. *The Mountain of Names: A History of the Human Family*. New York: Simon and Schuster, 1985.

SMITH, ELSDON C. *American Surnames*. Philadelphia: Chilton, 1969.

STRYKER-RODDA, HARRIET. *How to Climb Your Family Tree: Genealogy for Beginners*. Philadelphia and New York: J.B. Lippincott, 1977.

WESTIN, JEANE EDDY. *Finding Your Roots*. Los Angeles: J.P. Tarcher, 1977.

WIGGINTON, ELIOT. *Moments: The Foxfire Experience*. Washington, D.C.: Institutional Development and Economic Affairs Service, 1975.

ZEITLIN, STEVEN J., AMY J. KOTKIN, and HOLLY CUTTING BAKER. *A Celebration of American Family Folklore: Tales and Traditions from the Smithsonian Collection*. New York: Pantheon, 1982.

ACKNOWLEDGMENTS AND PHOTO CREDITS

My very special thanks to the fourth-grade students at Walter S. Boardman Elementary School in Oceanside, New York, who participated in the 1986–1987 pilot-project program *A Family History Workshop*. I want to express my gratitude to Bruce Misher, Principal; Ellen Goldberg, Language Arts Enrichment teacher; and Cynthia Johnson, Oceanside School District Elementary Library Consultant, for their gracious cooperation in making this program possible.

In addition, I want to thank Sarah Chester; the other faculty members of the exhibit staff; principal Donald Zwerling; and the students of the Edward Bleeker Junior High School in Flushing, New York, for having invited me to their 1987 Heritage Mini-Museum. I am especially grateful to those students who so generously shared with me their memories and experiences as both older and newer immigrants.

Photographs are from the collection of the author with the exception of the following, for which permission is gratefully acknowledged:

Smithsonian Institution National Anthropological Archives: page 7.
Solomon D. Butcher Collection, Nebraska State Historical Society: page 9.
Jessie Tarbox Beals, Jacob A. Riis Collection,
    Museum of the City of New York: page 12.
Lewis W. Hine Collection, New York Public Library: pages 15, 64.
Library of Congress: pages 31, 34, 61, 65, 66.
National Archives: pages 36, 50, 55.
New York Public Library: pages 44, 47.
National Park Service: pages 52, 58.
United Nations: page 68.
Lew Merrim (in the collection of the author): pages 81, 82.

❖➤➤➤ INDEX ➤➤➤❖

Italicized numbers indicate illustrations.

Index